The Compass to Financial Freedom

Navigate Your Path to Wealth

Andrew Galowey

Copyright © [Andrew Galowey] [2024]. All rights reserved. No part of this publication may be reproduced, distributed, or transmitted in any form or by any means, including photocopying, recording, or other electronic or mechanical methods, without the prior written permission of the publisher, except in the case of brief quotations embodied in critical reviews and certain other noncommercial uses permitted by copyright law.

Table Of Contents

Introduction

Chapter 1: Charting Your Course: Define Financial Freedom and Set Personalized Goals

Chapter 3: Taming the Tide: Building a Budget and Managing Debt

Chapter 4: Setting Sail: Savings Strategies and Creating an Emergency Fund

Chapter 5: Navigating the Open Seas: Exploring Wealth-Building Opportunities and Investing

conclusion

Introduction

Have you ever imagined a life free of financial worries? A life in which you may follow your interests, explore the globe, or just live comfortably without being confined to a desk? Financial independence is not a pipe dream; it is an attainable goal.

This book, "The Compass to Financial Freedom: Navigate Your Path to Wealth," will provide you with a tailored route to do precisely that. We'll look at not just the tools and tactics, but also how to apply them to your own objectives and circumstances. Whether you're just getting started or want to fine-tune your financial strategy, this book will provide you the information and confidence you need to design a route for a safe and rewarding future.

Here, you'll discover how to define financial independence for yourself, negotiate the often-confusing world of budgeting and debt management, and lay the groundwork for long-term wealth growth. We'll look at numerous investing possibilities and help you pick methods that match your risk tolerance and long-term objectives.

Set sail with us on this adventure to financial independence. This book is your compass, and together we'll steer you toward a better financial future.

Chapter 1: Charting Your Course: Define Financial Freedom and Set Personalized Goals

Imagine a life free of financial limitations. Imagine following your hobbies, touring the globe on your own schedule, or just living comfortably without the daily grind. This is not a utopian ideal; it is referred to as financial independence. But, before we get into the tools and tactics that will bring you there, this chapter is all about determining your own specific path.

Financial independence is not a one-size-fits-all idea. It's a personal place with a special significance for each person. For others, it may mean retiring early and pursuing hobbies. For others, it may be the opportunity to travel widely or start a successful company. The trick is to define your own definition of financial independence.

Finding Your True North: Define Financial Freedom

Ask yourself the following questions:

How would a perfect day in your financially free future look like? Are you working remotely from a beach in Bali? Are you spending quality time with your family without the stress of a busy job? Please describe your perfect daily routine.

What is your long-term goal? Do you want to establish a family, enhance your education, or leave a lasting legacy? Consider how finances influence your ability to achieve your objectives.

What are your fundamental values? Do you appreciate security and stability? Do you value experiences above material possessions? Understanding your values can help you make financial choices.

By answering these questions and thinking on your greatest aspirations, you begin to create a vivid image of your own financial independence.

Setting Personal Goals: A Roadmap to Success

Now that you have a better idea of where you want to go, you can start making a plan. Financial objectives should be S.M.A.R.T. (Specific, Measurable, Achievable, Relevant, and Timebound).

- particular: Don't just declare you want "more money." Set a particular financial goal, such as saving $10,000 for a down payment on a home within two years.

- Measurable: Be able to monitor your development. This might include developing a budget tracker or establishing milestones depending on percentages of your intended objective.

- Achievable: Be realistic about what you can do. Begin with smaller, more feasible objectives to gain momentum and confidence. As you succeed, you may progressively raise the difficulty.

- Relevant: Make sure your objectives are consistent with your broader vision of financial independence. Saving for a dream trip will be ineffective if you are deeply in debt.

Give yourself a timetable for completing each objective. This generates a feeling of urgency and keeps you motivated.

Beyond the Destination: Embrace the Journey

Financial independence is not achieved overnight. It's a journey that involves learning, changes, and sometimes setbacks. The idea is to enjoy the process, recognize minor accomplishments, and stay focused on your long-term goals. This book will provide you with the skills and methods you need to manage the trip, but the unique roadmap is up to you to build.

Action Steps:

Write out your notion of financial independence. Be precise and detailed.
Identify your long-term objectives and key values.
- Set your first S.M.A.R.T. financial objective and create a strategy to meet it.

Remember that your financial independence is waiting. This chapter is just the beginning of our journey to a better future. So grab your compass, buckle up, and let's go on this amazing voyage together!

Chapter 2: Calibrating Your Compass: Understanding Your Financial Environment

Congratulations! In Chapter 1, you laid out your strategy for achieving financial independence. Now it's time to calibrate your compass by knowing your existing financial status. Consider it like analyzing the weather before setting sail. Having a comprehensive view of your income, spending, obligations, and assets can help you make better financial choices going ahead.

Financial Literacy: The Foundation of Success

Financial literacy allows you to make educated financial decisions. This chapter will provide you with the necessary skills to confidently navigate your financial world.

Knowing Where You Stand: Tracking Income and Expenses

The first step is to understand your cash flow. Track your monthly revenue, including your salary, side hustles, and any other sources of cash. Then closely document your spending throughout the same time period. Every cent matters, so divide your expenses into three categories: necessary (rent, utilities, and food), discretionary (eating out, entertainment), and debt payments.

There are many different budgeting approaches. Popular budgeting methods include the 50/30/20 rule (allocating 50% for necessities, 30% for desires, and 20% for savings/debt repayment) and zero-based budgeting (allocating every dollar of revenue to a specified purpose). Find one that matches your spending patterns and follow it diligently. There are budgeting applications and spreadsheets available to make this process easier.

Understand Your Credit Report and Score

Your credit report is a complete record of your borrowing history, which includes loans, credit cards, and payment patterns. It has a big influence on your loan eligibility and interest rates. Request a free copy of your credit report from each of the three main credit agencies (Equifax, Experian, and TransUnion) every year. Examine it for correctness and identify any flaws that need fixing.

Your credit score is a three-digit number that reflects your creditworthiness. Higher scores mean better loan conditions and cheaper interest rates. Understanding your credit score and the elements that affect it is critical. A strong credit score is achieved by timely payments, low credit card usage (the ratio of your debt to your credit limit), and a diverse mix of credit instruments (loans and credit cards).

Taking Inventory of Assets and Liabilities

Assets are whatever you possess that is valuable, such as a vehicle, savings account, or home. Liabilities are your debts, such as credit card bills, school loans, and mortgages. To determine your net worth, remove your entire liabilities from your total assets.

Don't be disheartened if your net worth isn't where you want it to be yet. This is only a beginning point. By recording your income and spending, managing your credit, and implementing the ideas in this book, you will see your net worth slowly improve, indicating progress toward your financial objectives.

Face the Facts: Embracing Transparency

Understanding your financial condition, even if it isn't perfect, is critical. Avoiding the numbers will not result in their disappearance. Accept openness with yourself and identify places for growth. Perhaps you overpay on eating out or have a large credit card bill. Identifying these challenges is the first step toward effective transformation.

Action Steps:

Use a budgeting software or spreadsheet to keep track of your monthly income and spending.
- Choose a budgeting approach that is consistent with your spending patterns.
- Get a free copy of your credit report from each major credit agency and check it for accuracy.
- To calculate your net worth, remove your entire obligations from your total assets.

- Maintain honesty and transparency with yourself regarding your financial status.

Understanding your financial environment allows you to make more educated choices and take control of your financial destiny. This is the basis on which you will construct your journey to financial independence. In the next chapter, we'll look at debt-reduction tactics and how to create a viable budget, which are both critical stages on your road.

Chapter 3: Taming the Tide: Building a Budget and Managing Debt

Now that you've plotted your route and calibrated your compass (Chapters 1 & 2), it's time to address some of the most pressing challenges on your path to financial freedom: debt and uncontrolled spending. Consider your budget to be a ship; a well-constructed budget can withstand any financial storm. Effective debt management tactics can help you avoid extra difficulties and stay afloat.

Creating a Budget: Your Financial Roadmap

A budget is a financial plan that divides your income between costs and financial objectives. It's a road plan that assures you don't run out of steam (money) before reaching your goal (financial independence). Here's how to create a budget that works for you.

- Gather Your Information: Gather your most recent pay stubs, bank statements, and receipts. Understanding your revenue sources and normal spending is critical.

- Choose a Budgeting Method: Popular approaches include the 50/30/20 rule (50% necessities, 30% desires, 20% savings/debt) and zero-based budgeting (assigning each dollar a specific function). Experiment to discover a technique that fits your spending patterns.

- Divide your spending into categories such as rent or mortgage, utilities, food, transportation, entertainment, and debt payments.

- Monitor Your Spending: Be careful! Track your monthly expenses using a budgeting tool, spreadsheet, or basic notepad. This will identify areas where you may be overpaying.

- Analyze and Adjust: Once you've collected a month's worth of data, examine your spending patterns. Are you keeping to your budgeted amounts? Identify opportunities for improvement. Perhaps you might reduce your eating or entertainment expenses to free up funds for savings or debt payback.

- Be flexible but committed: Life occurs. Unexpected expenditures may occur. Review your budget on a regular basis and make adjustments as necessary. However, stick to your overall financial objectives.

Debt Management Strategies for Liberation

Debt may be a substantial impediment to financial independence. The good news is that there are effective ways for managing and eventually conquering it.

- Prioritize Your Debts: Not all debts are created equally. High-interest credit card debt should be addressed first due to compounding interest costs. To prioritize payments, list your loans from highest to lowest interest rates.

- The Debt Avalanche vs. Debt Snowball: The avalanche strategy emphasizes paying off the debt with the highest interest rate first, regardless of its size. The snowball strategy focuses on paying off the lowest debt first, regardless of interest rate, which may create a psychological sense of success. Choose the strategy that best aligns with your motivation and financial circumstances.

- Debt consolidation: Combining various debts into a single loan with a reduced interest rate may make payments easier and perhaps save money. Consider this option with care, ensuring that the total interest paid is lower and that you have a clear strategy for repaying the combined debt.

- Debt Negotiation: Contact your creditors to negotiate reduced interest rates or payback conditions, particularly for high-interest credit card debt. Explain your position and readiness to agree to a repayment plan. Persistence might be crucial to obtaining favorable conditions.

Consider strategies to enhance your income, such as starting a side business, doing freelance work, or negotiating a raise. This increased revenue may be dedicated straight to debt repayment, hastening the process.

Living within your means: breaking the cycle of overspending

Budgeting and debt management work hand in hand. A well-planned budget may help you prevent excessive debt buildup. Here are some methods to avoid overspending:

- Implement a "cooling-off" period: Wait 24 hours before making any impulsive purchases. Often, the urge diminishes, and you realize you don't really need the thing.
- Use cash for discretionary spending: Using cash to purchase non-essential products requires you to be conscious of your spending boundaries.
- Beware of lifestyle inflation: As your income rises, avoid the temptation to drastically raise your expenditure. Live

frugally and put the excess towards savings or debt reduction.
- Embrace free (or low-cost) entertainment: Go hiking, visit museums on free entry days, or have a picnic in the park.

Creating a manageable budget and properly managing your debt are critical steps toward financial independence. Taking charge of your money will allow you to save, invest, and achieve your long-term objectives. Remember that the road demands discipline.

Chapter 4: Setting Sail: Savings Strategies and Creating an Emergency Fund

Congratulations! You've plotted your path, calibrated your compass, and controlled the tides of debt (Chapters 1–3). It's time to set sail on your path to financial independence! This chapter emphasizes the significance of saving and creating a safe emergency fund, which will serve as your financial life raft in the event of an unforeseen storm.

The Power of Saving: Establishing Your Financial Foundation

Saving regularly is the foundation of financial independence. It enables you to create a safety net, attain financial objectives, and plan for the future. Here are important reasons to prioritize savings:

Peace of Mind: An emergency fund serves as a financial cushion for unforeseen situations such as auto repairs, medical expenses, or job loss. Knowing you have the means to withstand such storms alleviates tension and enables you to concentrate on solutions.

- Goal Achievement: Savings drive your capacity to fulfill financial objectives, whether they be for a down payment on a home, a dream trip, or supporting your child's school.

- Investing Opportunities: Savings pave the way for future investments. Once you've established a sufficient emergency fund, you may use the remainder to investigate wealth-building techniques such as stocks, bonds, or real estate.

Building an Emergency Fund: How Much Is Enough?

The optimal quantity for an emergency fund is determined by your specific needs. A decent rule of thumb is to save three to six months' worth of critical costs. If you have a steady income and few dependents, three months may enough. If you are self-employed or have a fluctuating income, aim for at least 6 months.

Savings Strategies: Making Every Penny Count

Here are some practical strategies to increase your savings:

- Automate Your Savings: Make automated payments from your checking account to your savings account every paycheck. This "pay yourself first" strategy promotes regular savings without depending on willpower.

- Use Multiple Savings Accounts: Consider setting up a high-yield savings account for your emergency fund. These accounts provide somewhat greater interest rates than typical savings accounts. However, keep these cash readily available in case of an emergency. For long-term objectives, consider alternatives such as retirement funds, which may provide tax benefits.

- Embrace the "No-Spend" Challenge: certain a goal for yourself to avoid needless spending for a certain length of time, such as a weekend or month. Redirect the savings to your emergency fund or other financial objectives.

- Review Subscriptions and ongoing Expenses: Examine your monthly invoices to locate any ongoing subscriptions or memberships that you no longer utilize. Cancelling these services may free up funds for saving.

- Sell Unused Possessions: To declutter your house, sell goods you no longer need via internet marketplaces or garage sales. Convert these discarded products into significant savings.

Beyond the emergency fund: Saving for specific goals

While an emergency fund is essential, consider creating different savings accounts for particular purposes, such as a down payment on a home or a dream trip. Categorizing your money helps you remain focused on attaining each goal.

Make Saving a Habit:

Saving consistently requires discipline. Here are some suggestions to make saving a habit:

- Track Your Progress: Seeing your funds increase over time is a tremendous motivation. Use budgeting applications or spreadsheets to track your progress and celebrate accomplishments.

- Set Realistic objectives: Begin with simple, attainable savings objectives and progressively expand them as you succeed. This increases confidence and momentum.

- Reward Yourself: Recognize yourself for accomplishing financial goals. This fosters good spending habits.

Saving regularly and creating a strong emergency fund are critical milestones on the road to financial independence. By prioritizing savings and using efficient techniques, you can weather financial storms and guarantee a better future. In the following chapter, we'll look at the fascinating realm of wealth creation via investing, including several tactics for long-term money growth.

Chapter 5: Navigating the Open Seas: Exploring Wealth-Building Opportunities and Investing

Congratulations! You've set your route, calibrated your compass, calmed the waves of debt, and established a solid emergency reserve (Chapters 1-4). Now it's time to set sail on the wide seas of money creation! This chapter delves into the fascinating world of investing, providing you with the knowledge and confidence to navigate various investment possibilities and increase your money in the long run.

Investing: Your Compass for Long-Term Growth

Saving regularly provides the groundwork for financial independence. Investing goes a step further, enabling your money to increase via a variety of assets such as stocks, bonds, and real estate. While there are associated hazards, investing has the potential to provide much larger returns than standard savings accounts.

Understanding Your Risk Tolerance

Before delving into particular investing possibilities, you must first assess your risk tolerance. Risk tolerance is your comfort level with prospective losses. Investors with a higher risk tolerance have the opportunity to generate bigger profits, but they also risk incurring greater losses. Conservative investors seek capital preservation and may choose lower-risk assets with lower expected returns.

Asset Allocation: Diversifying your Portfolio

Diversification is a key element in investing. Do not put all your eggs in one basket! Diversify your assets across asset groups to reduce risk. Common asset classes include:

Stocks: Stocks represent ownership in a firm and have the potential for significant development, but they also entail a larger risk.

- Bonds: Essentially loans to governments or firms, bonds provide consistent income and lower risk than equities.
- Real estate investing, whether in real property or Real Estate Investment Trusts (REITs), may generate both rental income and capital gain.
- Cash & Cash Equivalents: Low-risk solutions such as savings accounts or money market funds enable simple access to your money while yielding little returns.

By dividing your assets across asset classes depending on your risk tolerance and financial objectives, you may build a balanced portfolio that can grow while avoiding risk.

Exploring Investment Opportunities: A Sea of Possibilities

The financial environment provides a broad variety of alternatives. Here's a list of some common options:

- Individual Stocks: Investing in the stocks of certain firms enables you to possibly profit from their development. This method requires study and poses a greater risk.

- Mutual funds are professionally managed funds that pool money from different participants and invest in a diverse portfolio of assets such as equities and bonds. They provide a less expensive approach to diversify.

- Exchange-Traded Funds (ETFs): Like mutual funds, ETFs are passive investment vehicles that follow a specified index or sector. They have cheaper costs and better transparency than actively managed mutual funds.

- Retirement Accounts: Employer-sponsored plans, such as 401(k)s and Individual Retirement Accounts (IRAs), provide tax benefits for retirement savings. Contributions may grow tax-deferred or tax-free, depending on the account type.

- Alternative Investments: More experienced investors might consider real estate investment trusts (REITs), commodities (such as gold), or peer-to-peer lending. These need thorough investigation and pose varied degrees of danger.

Investment Strategies for Diverse Goals

Your investing plan should be personalized to meet your unique financial objectives and time frame. For short-term objectives, such as a down payment on a vehicle (within three years), lower-risk choices such as savings accounts or short-term bonds may be appropriate. For long-term objectives such as retirement (10 years or more), consider a growth-oriented portfolio with a greater equity allocation.

Investing for the Long Haul: Patience is Key

The stock market and other investment vehicles may be turbulent in the short run. Don't expect to become wealthy overnight. Investing is a marathon, not a sprint. Concentrate on a long-term plan, maintain discipline, and avoid making rash judgments based on market volatility.

Seeking professional guidance

While this book provides fundamental information, consider getting expert advice from a certified financial planner (CFP) for individualized investment plans. A CFP may evaluate your risk tolerance and financial objectives, and then offer appropriate investment solutions depending on your specific situation.

Investing has the ability to considerably increase your wealth and help you reach your financial objectives. Understanding your risk tolerance, diversifying your portfolio, and taking a long-term perspective can allow you to confidently traverse the vast seas of investing. Remember: information is power. Continue to study, be educated, and make sound investing choices to ensure your financial future. The quest to financial independence continues!

conclusion

You've reached the last chapter, which marks a watershed moment in your financial journey. This book has served as your compass, leading you through the sometimes murky seas of personal finance. We've discussed the necessity of developing your own vision of financial independence, the value of budgeting and debt management, and how to construct a solid emergency fund. Finally, we delved into the fascinating realm of investing, providing you with the information you need to navigate many possibilities and expand your money over time.

Remember that financial independence is a constant journey filled with learning, changes, and occasional course corrections. Consider this book to be your launchpad, pushing you towards a more prosperous financial future. The important thing is to be dedicated to your long-term goal. Review your objectives on a frequent basis, applaud accomplishments, and adjust your techniques as your circumstances change.

Lifelong learning is essential for this path. The financial environment is always evolving, so new investment possibilities may arise. To stay informed, read financial magazines, attend seminars, or talk with experienced specialists.

Most essential, empower yourself via educated financial choices. Don't be hesitant to seek advice from a professional financial planner who can customize methods to meet your individual goals and risk tolerance. Remember that information is power in the realm of money.

As you embark on this wonderful adventure, accept the obstacles and cherish your achievements. With steadfast determination, discipline, and the skills provided in this book, you may chart a route for a safe and rewarding financial future. The winds of financial independence await; set sail with confidence, and may your trip be fortunate!

www.ingramcontent.com/pod-product-compliance
Lightning Source LLC
Chambersburg PA
CBHW050249230526
45470CB00005B/2188